full Circle
The Story of Kent County's Millennium Park

First published in the United States of America in 2008 by the County of Kent, 300 Monroe Ave NW, Grand Rapids, Michigan 49503.

Published in part through the generosity of the Kent County Parks Foundation.

ISBN 13: 978-0-615-16257-7

Photography and copyright credits can be found on page 128.

This book was printed on Appleton Utopia U2:XG which is FSC-certified paper manufactured with electricity in the form of renewable energy (wind, hydro, and biogas), and includes a minimum of 30% post-consumer recovered fiber.

Table of Contents

Preface: Circle of Giving 6-13
  Jay Van Andel 8-9
  Millennium Park 10
  Founders' Circle 11
  Millennium Park Founders 12
  Millennium Park Pioneers 12
  Millennium Park Pathfinders 12
  Kent County Board of Commissioners 2000 13

Chapter 01 14-31
  A Sense of Place 16-18
  Timeline 19
  Roger Sabine, Peter Secchia, and Steve Heacock 20
  Pre-settlement Landscapes 21-23
  Landscape Character 1800 - 1900 24
  Landscape Character circa 1938 25
  Flora 26-27
  Norton Mounds Advisory Council 28
  Norton Mounds 29
  Floodplain 30-31

Chapter 02 32-55
  Reshaping the Land 34-36
  Timeline 37
  Grand Rapids Gravel and Dykema Excavators 38-39
  Natural Resources and
    Locations for Primary Industries 40
  Remnant Oil Pump 41
  Application to Drill 1939 42
  Land Permits 43
  Landscape 44-45
  Oil 46-47
  Gravel 48-49
  Gypsum 50-51
  George Seitsema, Property Owner 52-53
  Aerial Photograph of Millennium Park 54-55

Chapter 03 56-77
  Reclamation and Renewal 58-60
  Timeline 61
  Kent County Parks Foundation 62
  Sidwell Map 63
  Millennium Park Site 1999 64-65
  Site Preparation 2000-2002 66-70
  Millennium Park Master Plan 2003 71
  Construction 2002-2003 72-77

Chapter 04 78-103
  A Gift to the Future 80-82
  Timeline 83
  Public Beach 84
  Secchia Millennium Commission 85
  Directors, Local Foundation Contributors 86
  Public Beach 87
  2000 White House Millennium Council 88
  2004 Millennium Park Dedication 89
  Recreation Core: 2003 Master Plan 90
    Recreation Core Completed 91
    Splash Pad 92-93
    2006 Splash Pad 94
    2006 Park Shelters 95
    2006 Public Beach and Lake 96
    2006 Playground 97
    2006 Fishing and Observation Decks 98
    2006 Trails 99
    2006 Gathering Place 100-103

Chapter 05 104-123
  Completing the Vision 106-107
  The Millennium Standard 108
  The Millennium Park Vision 108
  Millennium Park 109
  Splash Pad 110
  Millennium Park Architectural Advisory Board 111
  Sustainable Design Committee 112
  Millennium Park 113
  Four Distinct Park Districts 114
    2006 Aerial View of Millennium Park 115
    Millennium Gateway Center 116
    Wild Flowers 117
    Boating Center 118
    The Fen 119
    Fred Meijer Millennium Trail Network 120-123
  A Circle Poem 124-125

Author's Note 126-127
Credits 128

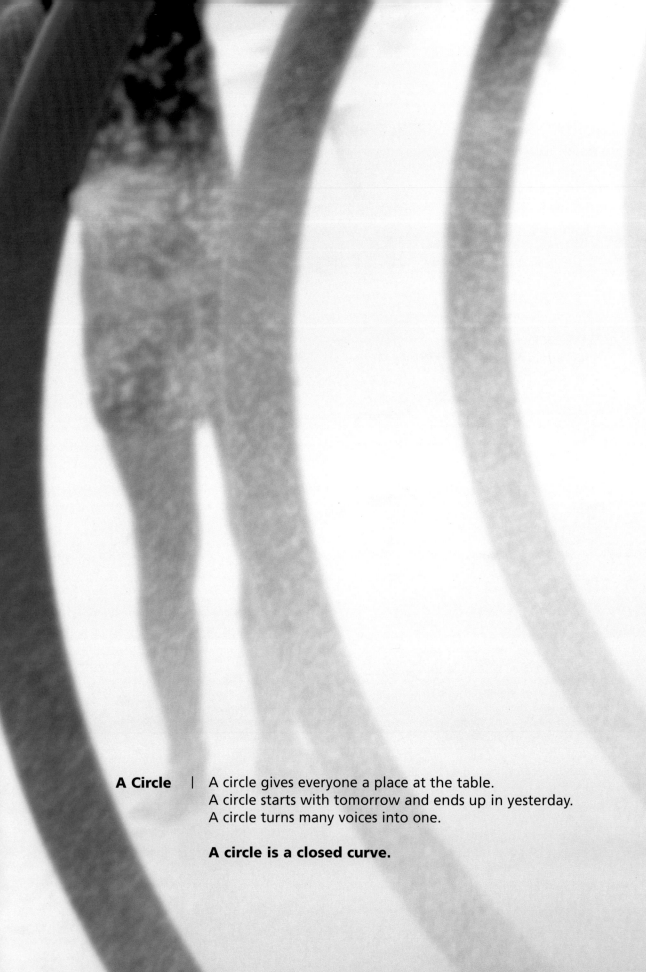

A Circle | A circle gives everyone a place at the table.
A circle starts with tomorrow and ends up in yesterday.
A circle turns many voices into one.

A circle is a closed curve.

FUTURE M.O

Grand
Rapids
Shines

Friends
Forever
2000

Steff
Caroline
Lindsey
Amie
Dan
Shannon
Amies
Katie
Alicia
Tara
Bri
Joanelle
Serene
Angela

Ryler
Kim
Matt
Jason
Sarah
Marcy

3G
Produ

Circle of Giving

Preface | In the beginning, Millennium Park was just a vision. A vision that sparked the imagination of a small circle of philanthropists, then caught fire and ignited a whole community.

Jay Van Andel
June 3, 1924 –
December 7, 2004

| Jay Van Andel was a lifelong supporter of this community. Millennium Park was just one of the many projects that benefited from his generosity. He was our friend, our advocate, and our benefactor. He believed in the power of this project, and any circle is incomplete without him.

John and Nancy Kennedy

Peter Wege

Frederik Meijer

Peter Secchia

Peter Cook

Mike and Sue Jandernoa

Richard DeVos

Founders' Circle | Millennium Park would not have been possible without the extraordinary vision and generosity of these very special donors. Early on, they understood how the park could contribute to the community, and then worked to make it a reality.

Our gratitude is endless.

Millennium Park Founders

In the year 2000, a small but committed group of major donors gave generous gifts to purchase land and provide start-up costs to create Millennium Park.

Peter C. and Pat Cook
The Richard and Helen DeVos Foundation
Fifth Third Bank
Frey Foundation
Charles Evenson Fund of the Grand Rapids
    Community Foundation
The Grand Rapids Press
John and Nancy Kennedy Family
Fred and Lena Meijer Family
Peter F. Secchia Family
Steelcase Foundation
Wege Foundation
The Citizens of Kent County, the City of Grand Rapids,
    and the City of Walker

Millennium Park Builders

After the initial land purchases were completed, this group of contributors donated funds to support construction of specific amenities within the park, helping to complete the original Millennium Park vision.

Peter C. and Pat Cook
The Richard and Helen DeVos Foundation
Frey Foundation
Harvey and Annie Gainey
Rollin M. Gerstacker Foundation
Grand Rapids Community Foundation
Grand Rapids Label Foundation
Dick and Sandy Hansen
Kenneth and Janice Hoexum
Mike and Sue Jandernoa
Sidney J. Jansma, Jr.
Keller Foundation
The Klopcic Family Foundation
Mehney Foundation/The KMW Group, Inc.
Meijer Foundation
National City Bank
Ginny Seyferth and Robert Boss Family
Jay and Betty Van Andel Foundation
James and Almeda Vander Waals Foundation
Warner Norcross and Judd LLP

Secchia Commission Executive Fundraising Committee

The Executive Fundraising Committee inspired and encouraged others to imagine the future, and developed the philanthropic support necessary to achieve the vision. These hardworking visionaries solicited millions of dollars in donations from the generous people of Kent County to make the dream of the park a reality.

Kimberly Bruyn
David Custer
Dan Gaydou
Robert Grooters
Barbara Hoag
Mike Jandernoa
Donald Maine
David Mehney
Dave Morren
Peter Secchia

Millennium Park Pioneers

As early contributors, the Pioneers helped make Millennium Park a reality. The citizens of West Michigan will never forget their shining example of generosity. Their leadership helped create one of the finest urban parks in America.

AJS Realty
Stephen J. Allen Family
Alticor
American Seating Company
Wm. Beckman Family
Blue Cross Blue Shield/Blue Care Network of Michigan
The Brooks Family Fund of the Community Foundation
    of the Holland/Zeeland Area
Comerica Bank
Crowe Chizek
Currie Family
Custer Office Environments
The People of Deloitte & Touche
Don and Ruth DeRuiter
The Dick and Betsy DeVos Foundation
DTE Energy Foundation
Ron and Carole Dykstra
Ernst & Young LLP
Bill Essling
Fehsenfeld Foundation
Fishbeck, Thompson, Carr & Huber, Inc.
Dan and Lou Ann Gaydou
Gordon Food Service
Gruel Mills Nims & Pylman LLP
G.R. Hansma Insurance
Steve and Brenda Heacock & Family
Jerry D. and Barbara J. Hoag
Irwin Seating Company
Mike and Sue Jandernoa Family
Keller Foundation
Charles W. Loosemore Foundation
Morris, Schnoor & Gremel
Owen-Ames-Kimball Co.
Louis and Helen Padnos Foundation
Chris and Joan Panopoulos
Pine Ridge Elementary
Jim and Marie Preston
Rehmann Robson, PC
Royce Rolls Ringer Co.
Sacred Heart Ladies Auxiliary
BDO Seidman, LLP
Seyferth Spaulding Tennyson Inc.
Brent and Diane Slay
Spartan Stores, Inc.
St. Andrew's School
Inta L. Grace and Lisa H. Story
Terryberry Company
Universal Forest Products Inc.

Standing – left to right: Jerry Kooiman, Beverly Rekeny, Paul McGuire, Jack Horton, Steven Heacock, Patrick Malone, Paul Mayhue, Kathy Kuhn, Elaine Buege, Jim Talen
Seated – left to right: Jack Boelema, Harold Mast, Tom Postmus, Ken Kuipers, Richard Smoke, Mike Sak, David Morren, Marv Hiddema, Fritz Wahlfield

Kent County Board of Commissioners 2000

This group was responsible for approving the original Millennium Park proposal on behalf of Kent County and allocated the initial $14.5 million in county funds to acquire land for the park. Their support for the vision – their willingness to turn *what could be* into *what will be* – has earned them a unique place in our community's history. Their legacy is the pleasure of generations of park visitors.

01

To This Place | There is a mystery to this place.
Even the stones
Have their secrets.

Lovers and warriors tell their tales
And the shards have a voice
If you know how to listen.

Yet the stones are silent.
Keeping their watch
Over every new way.

We only know what we are told.
But the rest is there
At the bottom of the river.

A Sense of Place

Chapter 01 | The area that would become Millennium Park is located on the floodplain of the Grand River. The environment that exists today began around 20,000 years ago when the glaciers began to melt and retreat from Michigan's Lower Peninsula. As the glaciers withdrew, they left behind the deposits of crushed rock, sand, silt, and clay that made the area excellent for gravel mining.

Norton Mounds Mural, Courtesy of the Public Museum of Grand Rapids, Michigan

Pottery shards recovered from the College of Michigan excavations in 1963-64, Courtesy of the Public Museum of Grand Rapids, Michigan

Historians date the presence of humans in Michigan to nearly 12,500 B.C., yet it wasn't until 100 B.C. that Western Michigan was inhabited by native peoples. As of 10 B.C., the Norton Mounds site was only one of several mound groups that were constructed by the Hopewell peoples, probably as part of an annual celebration. The mounds were named after the owner on whose property the burial mounds were first excavated. Categorized today as "prehistoric peoples," the Hopewells gathered on the banks of the Grand River in the Grand River Valley to celebrate life, mourn the dead, and pray for blessings for the New Year. The mounds were used until about 200 A.D., when the peoples abandoned Western Michigan and moved elsewhere.

Until the early 19th century, the mounds remained untouched. In 1836, renowned Grand Rapidian John Ball noted a group of mounds in his travels around the area. Then, possibly intrigued by Ball's findings, W.L. Coffinberry came to Grand Rapids in the 1870s to explore the strange mounds; later, in 1893, he excavated six of the 13 mounds. Coffinberry's findings recognized the mounds as historically significant, which led to a handful of other amateur excavations. In 1921, the City of Grand Rapids officially passed the first deed to acknowledge and protect the mounds, claiming "that the Indian Mounds Park will be adequately protected from vandalism, and made attractive so that it shall always remain as a historic memorial of the Native Americans."

Before the year 2000, the mounds would become National Historic Landmarks, be placed on the National Register of Historical Places, and be overseen by The Norton Mounds Advisory Council. As prominent historical artifacts, they have been studied and examined by countless historians and archeologists, giving a glimpse into the early history of Grand Rapids. As symbols of Native American heritage, they have been both protected by local Native American officials and brought under the conservation of the Public Museum of Grand Rapids.

Chapter 01 | Timeline

12,500 B.C. — Humans enter the Lower Peninsula of Michigan.

100 B.C. — The prehistoric Hopewell peoples arrive in upper Great Lakes Region.

10 B.C. — First mounds built in area (proven through carbon dating).

1836 — Prominent Grand Rapids resident John Ball notes 20 mounds in an account of his travels.

1876 — W.L. Coffinberry publishes his explorations of the mounds.

1893 — Coffinberry excavates six of the mounds.

1915 — Excavations of the mounds by H.E. Sargent, Director of Kent Scientific Museum.

1921 — Mounds area deeded to City of Grand Rapids; quit-claim deed "provided further, that the Indian Mounds Park will be adequately protected from vandalism, and made attractive so that it shall always remain as a historic memorial of the Native Americans."

1935 — *Grand Rapids Press* article states mounds are in unkempt condition.

1936 — Mounds officially become city property and are named the Norton Mounds Group.

1936 — Mounds mapped by City Engineer, Edmond P. Gibson.

1950s — City erects roadside signs marking the mounds, installs a gravel road, clears the area of poison ivy and trash.

1952 — Carroll family transfers land circumscribing mounds to the city.

1957 — Norton Mounds Group formally recognized and listed on the Michigan State Register of Historic Sites.

1964 — Mounds excavated by College of Michigan and Grand Valley State College archeologists. The most important excavation unearthed a total of 35 skeletons (four intact).

1965 — Mounds designated National Historic Landmarks, one of only 2500 sites nationwide.

1966 — Mounds listed on the National Register of Historical Places.

1971 — Public Museum of Grand Rapids begins moving forward with development studies and proposals regarding the Norton Indian Mounds Park and Interpretive Center.

1975 — Board of Art and Museum Commissioners issues resolutions to retain all mound artifacts in the museum's care and to return all historic human remains to the Native American community for reburial.

1982 — Fence erected around mounds to reduce vandalism and trash dumping.

1999 — Public Museum of Grand Rapids initiates Norton Mounds Cultural Resource Project; hires Debra Muller as Project Manager.

Roger Sabine, Peter Secchia, and Steve Heacock

If a park can have Founding Fathers, these three are ours. We are grateful for their vision, influence, and tenacity. Truly, Millennium Park would not exist without them.

Roger Sabine, Kent County Parks Director, understood how depleted industrial land could become a jewel of the park system. Peter Secchia, philanthropist and former Ambassador to Italy, chaired the Millennium Commission that identified and promoted the park project as a lasting gift to future generations. He has remained one of Millennium Park's most tireless and enthusiastic advocates. Steve Heacock chaired the Kent County Board of Commissioners when they made the landmark decision to accept and fund the Millennium Park project proposal. At the same time, the Board placed renewed emphasis on the Kent County parks system and embarked upon an aggressive parkland purchase program.

Sluiceway in Spring

High Riparian Terrace

Sluiceway Discharge Wetland

Floodplain

Fish Farm Fen

Pre-settlement Landscapes | In several locations, scientists have been able to identify a handful of "pre-settlement landscapes," which have withstood two centuries of industrial use. These landscapes include woodlands, wetlands, marshland, swamps, and "fens," where water is seeping out of the ground on a gentle slope. They contain 95 percent of the species of plants native to Kent County that reside within Millennium Park and are considered some of the finest remnant landscapes along the entire Grand River.

Triangle Woodland

Riparian Terrace

Sluiceway Woodland

Wooded Seep

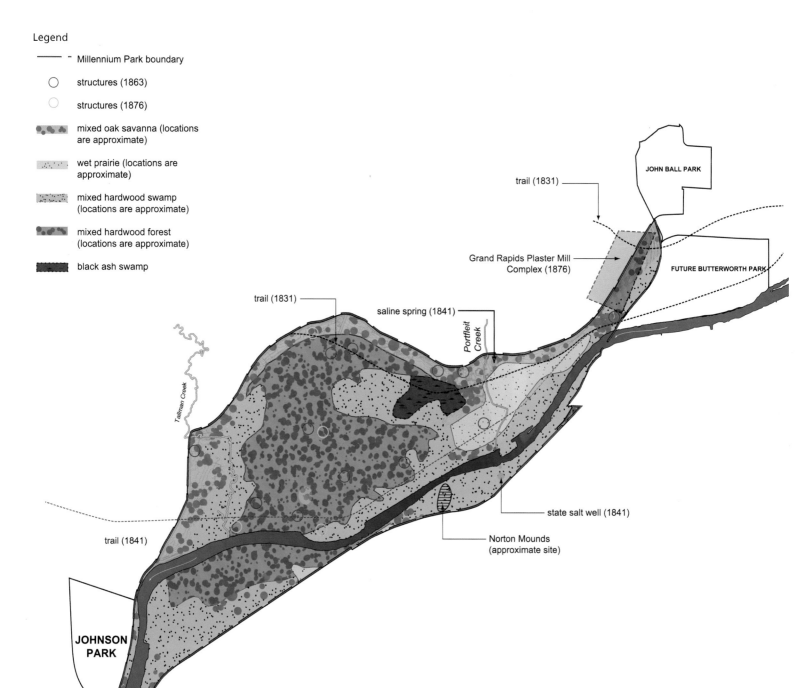

Legend

- — ‑ Millennium Park boundary
- ○ structures (1863)
- ○ structures (1876)
- mixed oak savanna (locations are approximate)
- wet prairie (locations are approximate)
- mixed hardwood swamp (locations are approximate)
- mixed hardwood forest (locations are approximate)
- black ash swamp

JOHN BALL PARK

trail (1831)

Grand Rapids Plaster Mill Complex (1876)

FUTURE BUTTERWORTH PARK

trail (1831)

saline spring (1841)

Portfleit Creek

Tallman Creek

state salt well (1841)

Norton Mounds (approximate site)

trail (1841)

JOHNSON PARK

Landscape Character 1800 - 1900 | This map illustrates the pre-settlement native plant communities within the park. At that time, the site was a tapestry of mixed oak savanna, wet prairie, mixed hardwood swamp, mixed hardwood forest, and black ash swamp.

Legend

— – Millennium Park boundary

BW   Bluff Woodland

MA   Marsh

TW   Terrace Woodlands

SW   Swamp

Notes:
1. Absence of mining and oil wells.

Sources:
1. 1939 Aerial provided by Kent County NRCS office.

Landscape Character | This map represents the character of the landscape in the
circa 1939   late-1930s, when two agricultural settlements existed within
the park boundaries. Two small parcels were used for
row-crop farming; the majority of the area was used for
less intensive farming and pasture land. At that time, there
were still trails used by Native Americans in the approximate
location of Butterworth Drive.

Flora | Millennium Park features an extremely biodiverse environment. An important goal of the park is to protect, preserve, and restore the habitat for native plants and animals.

"The park land also originally was home to a wide array of animals, including white-tailed deer, elk, raccoon, squirrels, rabbits, fox, turkey, skunks, opossum, coyote, passenger pigeon, hawks, owls, woodpeckers, and cardinals." *

* The Norton Mounds Site: A description and history of a prominent cultural national historic landmark, compiled by Commonwealth Cultural Resources Group, Inc., under contract with the Public Museum of Grand Rapids.

From left, back row: Christian Carron, Janet Brashler, John Halsey, David Medema (guest), Mark Vysoky, James McClurken, Erik Alexander, Jeff Gartner (guest), Jim Mulder. Middle row, from left: Paula Gangopadhyay, Julie Stivers (guest), Lori Shustha, Dan Shepherd, Timothy Chester, Fran Pepper, Shirley Francis, Benjamin Williams, W.D. Frankforter, Debra Muller, Mark Fitzpatrick. Front kneeling: Roger Williams, left and Dan Rapp.

Courtesy of the Public Museum of Grand Rapids, Michigan. Photographer, Thomas Kachadurian

| Norton Mounds Advisory Council | The Norton Mounds Advisory Council was convened by the Public Museum of Grand Rapids in 2002 to assist the community in preserving this historic site. The Council includes members from the local community and national level of Native American nations, as well as scientists, historians, educators, government officials and other expert stakeholders. |

Norton Mounds | The Norton Mounds are sacred burial grounds left behind by the Hopewell peoples, an ancient civilization that flourished over 2,000 years ago. The Hopewell culture was vast and developed in response to the abundant natural resources, plants, and animal life in this area. The Norton Mounds site consists of 13 conical mounds, the largest of which is 15 feet high and 80 feet in diameter. The mounds are prominent and obvious features along the flat floodplain of the Grand River, southwest of downtown Grand Rapids. Millennium Park includes the Norton Mounds site within its borders.

02

So Much Here | Everything is here.

We are still young,
The builders and dreamers
And the men with money.

We have not learned what they learned.

There is only
So much here.

Reshaping the Land

Chapter 02 | The Millennium Park area has been used by human beings for millennia, first by native peoples, and beginning in the 1830s, by European American settlers. These settlers farmed along the inviting banks of the Grand River, despite the fact that most of the site was, and is, within a floodplain. Although both Native American peoples and settlers discovered salt wells in the area, the first significant commercial use of the land was gypsum mining. This industry, with its end-use applications in plaster and wallboard, existed from 1827 through 2000, when the last manufacturing facility on Butterworth Drive closed its doors. Along with gypsum mining came a thriving mushroom industry, as the dark, cool, and dry mines were discovered to be an excellent environment for growing.

While gypsum mining produced a vast unseen network of underground tunnels, the gravel mining industry was largely responsible for shaping the distinct Millennium Park landscape visible today. The mined areas are all below the water table and have created many shallow water bodies throughout the park. Gravel mining, begun in the 1930s by Grand Rapids Gravel Company, continued for more than 80 years, a testament to the vast reserves of sand and gravel once contained within the park.

In the late 1930s, Grand Rapids experienced somewhat of an oil boom, following the success of a wildcat well near Johnson Park. At its peak, the oil field included some 150 active wells within a 4.5-mile area to the west of the city. Today, more than 50 operating wells can be found within the park boundaries.

Chapter 02 | Timeline

1831-1837 — Land surveys indicate two settlements within the park area.

1838 — Salt well is authorized by state legislature on Norton site.

1839-1841 — Salt well in full operation on Norton site.

1841 — First gypsum discovered near Plaster Creek.

1842 — Kent established as a county.

1849 — R.E. Butterworth opens a small gypsum quarry, which he sold to Hovey & Company in 1856.

1850 — Grand Rapids established as a city.

1852 — The first gypsum mine opens in Walker Township. Gypsum shipments reach upwards of 60 tons daily.

1860 — Grand Rapids Plaster Company opens.

1863 — R.E. Butterworth opens short-lived oil refinery in Grand Rapids.

1869 — Chicago and Michigan Lake Shore Railroad reaches city in 1869; railroad corridor passes within 250 feet of easternmost mound.

1907 — American Cement and Plaster Company begins to quarry in the area.

Early 1920s — Grand Rapids Gravel Company acquires land near the Norton site.

1928 — Northern Oil & Gas Company opens facilities in Kent County.

1929 — First oil and gas lease let to Rex Oil and Gas Company.

1930s — Gravel quarrying begins in Grand Rapids. Oil is found in the Walker-Tallmadge oil field in Walker Township.

1935 — WPA riverside development and beautification project on south bank of Grand River approved for $1.2 million; becomes Indian Mounds Drive.

1938-1942 — Walker Oil Field produces 3,476,736 barrels.

1946 — Abandoned Michigan Gypsum Company land purchased by Kragt family; used as an underground storage facility.

1951 — More than a million tons of gravel scooped out of Walker Township.

1960s — Construction of I-196 through landscape; highway moved far enough south to miss the mound group.

2000 — All gypsum mining operations in Grand Rapids area closed down.

Approximately 130 oil wells – both active and capped – remain within the park boundaries.

From left: Andy Dykema, Dykema Excavators and Dan Schimmel, Grand Rapids Gravel Company

Grand Rapids Gravel and Dykema Excavators | Grand Rapids Gravel Company and Dykema Excavators were early partners in the Millennium Park project. The acquisition of several hundred acres of mined land with lakes adjacent to Johnson Park was the impetus for a dramatic expansion of the Kent County parks system. These parcels became the cornerstone for the future Millennium Park.

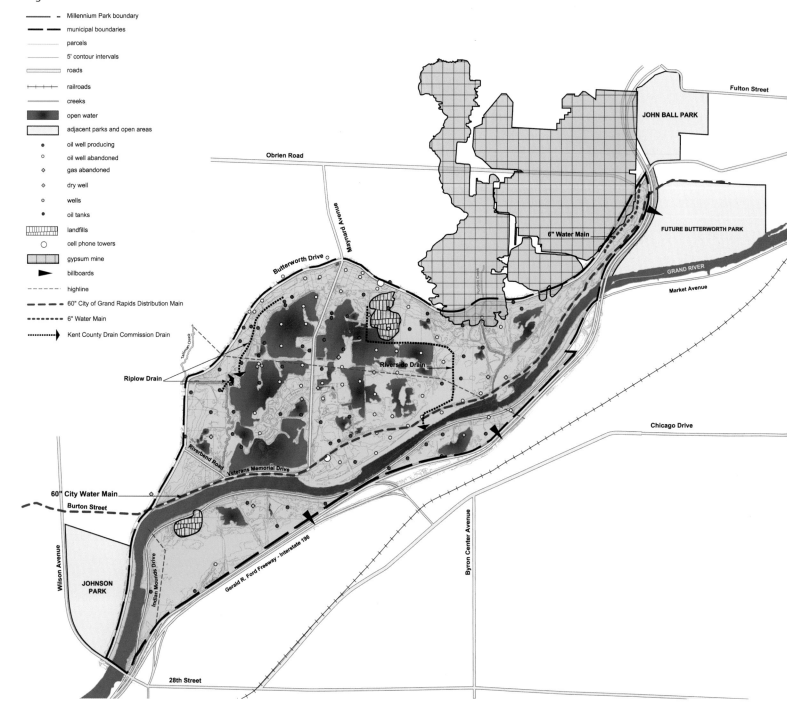

Legend

- — · Millennium Park boundary
- — — municipal boundaries
- parcels
- 5' contour intervals
- roads
- ┼┼┼┼ railroads
- creeks
- open water
- adjacent parks and open areas
- • oil well producing
- ○ oil well abandoned
- ◇ gas abandoned
- ◇ dry well
- ○ wells
- • oil tanks
- landfills
- ○ cell phone towers
- gypsum mine
- ► billboards
- - - - - highline
- — — 60" City of Grand Rapids Distribution Main
- · · · · 6" Water Main
- · · · ► Kent County Drain Commission Drain

Natural Resources and Locations for Primary Industries | Many sites within the current Millennium Park boundaries were used commercially from the mid-1800s through the 20th century. Salt extraction and gypsum mining were among the first uses; eventually, on-site operations processed drywall and other products. The oil industry exploded in the late 1930s, setting off a mini-boom that resulted in hundreds of active wells in the area. Many wells are still in operation today. More recently, sand and gravel mines provided materials for road construction, concrete, and other building materials. Predictably, as these industries prospered, the area was also used to landfill various materials no longer needed.

∠19-39
∠↗

STATE OF MICHIGAN
DEPARTMENT OF CONSERVATION
APPLICATION FOR PERMISSION TO DRILL
AN OIL, GAS OR TEST WELL
PERMIT FEE OF $25.00 TO BE PAID BY BANK DRAFT, CERTIFIED
CHECK, MONEY ORDER OR CASH MUST ACCOMPANY APPLICATION

PROTECT LIFE -- DRILL IN CAREFULLY

Date...... April 19, ... 19 39

Lessee ...... Swanson Consolidated Oil Company ......
Owner or operator

Address...... Alma, Michigan ......

Farm ...... John Fletcher ...... Well No. ...... 2 ......
Full name of owner of fee

The number of acres contained in the lease ...... 1/2 acre ......

...... SE 1/4 of the ...... SW 1/4 of the ...... SE 1/4 of Sec.32 ...... T 7N. R. 12W

Township ...... Walker ...... County ...... Kent ......

Locate well in two directions from the NEAREST quarter-section and property lines:

195 ft. from north/south line of quarter sec. 760 ft. from east/west line of quarter sec.

66 ft. from north/south property line. 83 ft. from east/west property line.

...... 460± ...... ft. from nearest well.

Kind of tools to be used ...... Cable ...... Intended depth of well ...... 1875'
Cable, rotary, combination

Date actual drilling is to start ...... Apr. 22, 1939 Purpose of well ...... Oil
Oil, gas, test hole

Name of drilling contractor ...... R. A. Wells ......

Has applicant filed surety bond covering operations? ...... Yes ...... If so give expiration date 7-15-39
Yes or No

Formations expected to be penetrated: Method to be used in protecting fresh water, valuable brines, or mineral deposits: Method to be used in controlling well upon completion ...... To drill into Traverse; 10 inch drive pipe through drift; 8½ inch casing set through Marshall at about 400' and cemented with enough material to come to top of hole; 6-5/8 inch casing to be set and cemented through the Berea. 5-3/16" casing to be set and cemented on top of Traverse; well to be equipped with control head and master gate valve when drilling into or through any oil or gas formation; every possible precaution to be taken.

Applicant (Lessee) agrees to properly and adequately dispose of all brines and oil wastes and to conform with all fire regulations.

(Signed)...... Swanson Consolidated Oil Co. ...... By ...... Leonard R. Ward ......

Office address ...... Alma, Michigan ...... Phone No. ...... 158 ......

Name of person to whom correspondence is to be s ...... Mr. Leonard F. Ward ......

Address ...... same ...... Phone No. ......

Permit No. 6068 ...... Issued ...... April 19, ... 19 39 ......

P. J. Hoffmaster
Supervisor of Wells

By ...... L. M. Gorsline ......

SECTION PLAT (640 AC)
LOCATE WELL & LEASE ACCURATELY

NOTE:—If property is irregular in form or less than 5 acres, attach legal description by metes and bounds together with large scale sketch giving dimensions and distances in feet.

Land Permits | The State of Michigan requires oil well owners to obtain permits before drilling. This permit, issued in 1939 to Swanson Consolidated Oil Company, allowed the owner to drill down to 1,875 feet. In April of that year, Swanson produced 3,300 barrels per day from wells in the Walker oil field.

Oil | On October 24, 1938, Detroiters Bryon MacCallum and George Herr hit oil at their wildcat well in Walker Township near Johnson Park. By 1939, Kent County was considered the second-largest oil-producing county in Michigan. In only one year, the county had produced more than one million barrels of oil at the Walker oil field, which is now partially within the current Millennium Park boundaries. At its peak, the Kent County oil boom was fueled by over 700 active wells within a 4.5-mile area. For a brief period, the Furniture City became the Oil City. By 1941, the area's once-booming crude oil output had declined dramatically, and many wells were abandoned. Today, the industry consists of only a handful of small-yield wells.

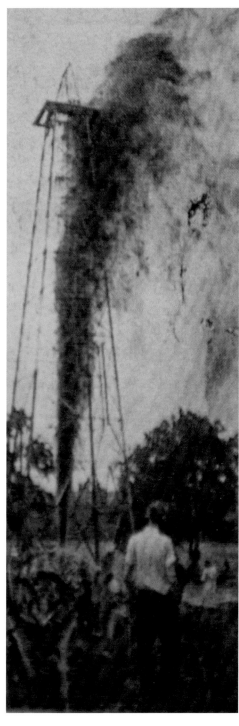

Gravel | Thanks to its unique geology and riverbank setting, Grand Rapids is blessed with a large number of high-yield gravel deposits. Local pits have supplied the crushed rock needed for the community's roads, driveways, sidewalks, and other infrastructure. Gravel mining is a complex process, requiring surveying, site clearing, excavation, stripping, washing, processing, and shipping. Mining companies must invest heavily in equipment, processing, and transportation – and mined land must be reclaimed and redirected to other uses once the gravel has been depleted. Gravel mining is still a thriving industry in the Grand Rapids area, furnishing the tons of sand and gravel aggregate needed to support the region's economic development. Long-distance transportation of construction-grade gravel is virtually impossible; mining operations must be located near high-usage metropolitan areas.

Gypsum | Furniture manufacturing earned Grand Rapids a national reputation, but it was not the first industry to make its mark on the local economy. For decades, Grand Rapids was the center of a thriving but little-known industry: *gypsum mining*. Deep underneath the metropolitan area is a labyrinth of cool, dry gypsum mines. These mines were in operation from 1841 (on Plaster Creek) until 2000, when the last Butterworth Drive facilities were closed and sealed. Gypsum mining operations were largely confined to the northeastern portion of the current Millennium Park.

Grand Rapids' first real gypsum entrepreneur was R.E. Butterworth, who discovered gypsum in 1849 while plowing a field, and in 1852, built a plaster mill on what is now Butterworth Drive. The operation at this site later became Eagle Mills Plaster Company, then Grand Rapids Plaster Company. In 1877, the company was also the location of one of the first telephones in Grand Rapids, a gift from Alexander Graham Bell to his friend William Hovey, President of Hovey & Company and eventually one of the owners of Grand Rapids Plaster.

In the early years, gypsum was used primarily for fertilizer or "land plaster." As America prospered, so did the gypsum industry, ultimately providing plaster for wallboard and many other household, medical, and construction applications. Eventually, as the tunnels were abandoned, their constant low temperatures and humidity made them an excellent location for commercial storage.

George Seitsema, | George Seitsema was one of the landowners who sold his
Property Owner | property to Kent County for the new Millennium Park. He
requested that the gravel pit near his home – now a lake –
be named after his late wife, Leota.

First Known Aerial Photograph of Millennium Park Area (undated) | The first aerial photographs of the Millennium Park area were taken after 1938. This undated photo is looking southeast across the Grand River. The road following the river is now Indian Mounds Drive and the road across the top third of the photo is Chicago Drive (with Byron Center Avenue heading south). In the 1960s, Interstate 196 would be built parallel to and between the two roads, slightly south of the historic Norton Mounds.

03

What the Land Asks | Never mind the tunnels and the towers
And the broken green glass.
No one needs your apologies.
I have already forgiven you,
As the swollen river forgives the spring rain.
What I ask is much harder.
Give me back
Only what you have taken.
The darkness, the silence
And the laughter of a child.

Reclamation and Renewal

Chapter 03 | Three years before the Millennium, Grand Rapids Gravel contacted Kent County Parks, requesting to mine fifty acres of land adjacent to Johnson Park. In return, Grand Rapids Gravel would give the county 150 acres of mined land, also located near Johnson Park, most likely to be used as "green space." A campaign was formed, and the county began to allocate money and land acquisition funds.

One year before the Millennium, under the leadership of Peter Secchia, the Millennium Commission was formed. The Commission was part of a national movement to celebrate the Millennium with large-scale community projects. The newly acquired land caught their eye. Within months, the Millennium Park plan was approved and the groundwork was laid. Formal fundraising began strongly with a $2,000,000 gift from the Commission and $250,000 from local philanthropist Peter Wege.

Millennium Park was proposed with a twenty-year plan. The public beach was opened in 2003. In 2004, Phase 1 was completed and marked with a formal dedication and the opening of the "Splash Pad."

Chapter 03 | Timeline

1976 — 26-acre land parcel is deeded to city by Grand Rapids Gravel Company, with the stipulation that the land be used only for park purposes.

1977 — City purchases additional land owned by Rocks Redi-Mix Company.

1992 — Kent Trails, a 15-mile, non-motorized trail that is the result of a collaborative planning effort between the Kent County Parks Department and four adjacent cities, is opened using Indian Mounds Drive.

1997 — Grand Rapids Gravel Company inquires about mining a 50-acre parcel of Kent County-owned land, offering to exchange 150 acres of mined-out land with lakes adjacent to the existing Johnson Park.

1998 — As the county's interest in securing additional park land for nature conservation grows under Chair Steven Heacock, Kent County allocates $4 million for land acquisition. Plans are formed to extend Johnson Park with the Grand Rapids Gravel Company land.

1999 — The all-volunteer, non-profit Kent County Parks Foundation is established to support the mission of the Kent County Parks Department to establish, maintain, and expand outstanding public parks and to preserve open space.

The City of Grand Rapids and Kent County appoint the Secchia Millennium Commission; Peter Secchia, former Ambassador to Italy, chairs. Commission is charged with identifying high-impact projects to celebrate the new Millennium.

Building on the Parks Department's vision of an expanded Johnson Park, the Secchia Millennium Commission recommends selection of a large urban park as the community's "commemorative gift."

A Master Plan for a Johnson Park Extension is developed for the Kent County Parks Commission. The plan explored the possibility of creating a water-oriented county park that incorporated the land formed by ongoing mining operations into a recreation landscape.

Left to right: Christopher Machuta, Treasurer; Barbara J. Hoag, President; Stephen J. Mulder, Secretary

Kent County Parks Foundation | The all-volunteer Kent County Parks Foundation was established in 1999 – as the Millennium Park project was taking shape – to assist in finding funds for park improvement and expansion. The Foundation has been a steady presence throughout the planning and implementation of the park.

Sidwell Map | The Millennium Park vision began with a public-private partnership between Kent County and Grand Rapids Gravel Company to extend Johnson Park. In these 1998 maps, the parcels that were part of the original discussions for park expansion are outlined. This transaction was the springboard for the entire Millennium Park project.

Millennium Park Site | 1999

This aerial photo documents the future Millennium Park location, just west of downtown Grand Rapids, prior to the start of site preparation. The area was heavily mined for gravel and sand for many years; this shot shows the network of small ponds created by quarries that have filled with groundwater. The photo testifies to the size and scale of this unique and ambitious project.

The park site incorporates land located in the Cities of Grand Rapids, Wyoming, Walker, and Grandville. It includes nearly five miles of Grand River frontage.

**Site Preparation
2000-2002**

| The development of the proposed park required extensive site preparation. Pre-construction activity, including earth moving and gravel mining, went on simultaneously with public and private fundraising and land acquisition.

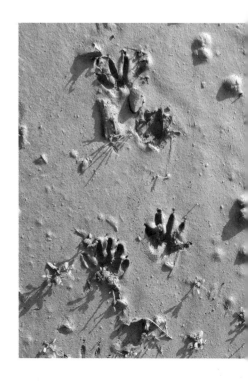

**Millennium Park
Master Plan
2003**

Phase I of the park focused on 200 acres of land that included a 100-acre, man-made lake.

In Relationship to Other Kent County Parks
The Millennium Park site is located outside of Grand Rapids, between Johnson Park to the west and John Ball Zoological Garden to the east. The park is directly connected to the Kent Trails network, making it possible to safely enter the park without driving or walking along roadways.

**Construction
2002-2003** | Phase I of the massive construction project began with work to transform the gravel pits into a landscaped site featuring a beach house, swimming beach, and fishing ponds with wooden deck overlooks – all handicap accessible.

Brick walkways lead past picnic pavilions to a bridge and beach house, all of which feature concrete, light wood, and cut limestone columns. A metal archway stands in front of the Van Andel beach house that leads to a signature clock tower.

04

**Where the
Children Play** | This is sacred space
Where the children play
A snow snake, a piece of string
Artifacts of lasting grace.

Perhaps at this place
We were meant to see
The intersection of faith
And the cruelty of time.

A Gift to the future

Chapter 04 | Phase I of Millennium Park was the result of a partnership between Kent County and the Secchia Millennium Commission. Fundraising for the multi-year project began with a $3 million grant approved by the Kent County Board of Commissioners on March 23, 2000. This first phase of the project was estimated to cost $5 million; the total project cost was estimated at $20 million over ten years and will eventually include 1500 acres.

The resolution authorizing the grant also approved in concept an agreement with Grand Rapids Gravel Company to acquire 350 acres of depleted land, formerly used for gravel mining. It also acknowledged the Secchia Millennium Commission's commitment to raise $2 million in private funding for the project. General fundraising began in earnest on Earth Day, April 20, 2000. Under Ambassador Secchia's leadership, the Commission initially raised close to $4 million in private funds to begin acquisition and development of the park. Through the community's continuing generosity this total now stands at nearly $13 million.

The initial goal of the Millennium Park project was to develop a greenway-type urban space connecting Johnson Park on the west end and John Ball Park on the east. Phase I included 200 acres stretching along the Grand River to the far western end of the park. Called the Recreation Core, this area's focal point was a pristine 100-acre lake and sandy beach formed from an old quarry. Phase I was an immediate, popular success, attracting hundreds of visitors in its first month of operation (August 2003). The park was officially dedicated at a community celebration on July 2, 2004.

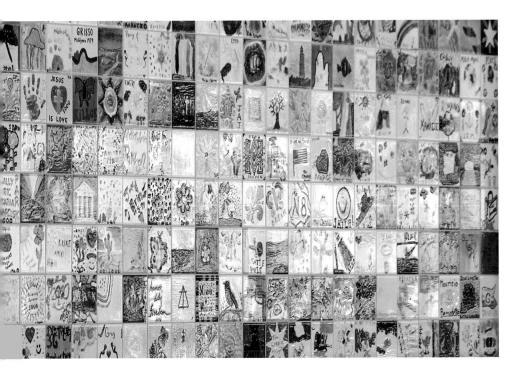

Chapter 04 | Timeline

2000 — The large urban park project is approved by the Kent County Board of Commissioners and named Millennium Park. Board commits $3 million for the project.

The Secchia Millennium Commission pledges to raise $2 million in private funding for the project. They raise $3.7 million.

The Millennium Park project is designated an official project of the White House Millennium Council.

The Secchia Millennium Commission "Miles of Tiles" project, a colorful wall mosaic created from 2000 clay tiles painted by residents around the theme of "honor the past and imagine the future," begins.

Michigan Department of Natural Resources Foundation commits $2,360,000.

2001 — Original Millennium Park Master Plan is developed.

2001-2003 — Site preparation and construction of Phase I park features begin.

2003 — Phase I, the park's Recreation Core, informally opens to visitors in August.

2004 — Millennium Park officially opens in a gala dedication ceremony and community celebration on July 2.

2004 — Peter Secchia is named "Outstanding Contributor" for his tireless work and "contagious enthusiasm" on behalf of Millennium Park.

Ambassador Secchia helps raise more than $8 million in private funds for land acquisition and development of the new park.

Secchia Millennium Commission |

The Secchia Millennium Commission was appointed by Kent County and the City of Grand Rapids to celebrate the year 2000 with various community events and activities. The primary mission of the Commission became the designation of a major project to benefit future generations of Kent County residents. The park project was selected and named Millennium Park by the Kent County Board of Commissioners.

The Secchia Millennium Commission made a commitment to raise $2 million by Earth Day in April 2001, but actually raised close to $4 million by the deadline. Due to their initial success, the team decided to increase the private-sector fundraising goal to $5 million.

From left: Ellen Satterlee, Wege Foundation; Diana Sieger, Grand Rapids Community Foundation; Milt Rohwer, Frey Foundation; Susan Broman, Steelcase Foundation

Directors, Local Foundation Contributors | Local foundations quickly stepped up to support the Millennium Park project. Their funding provided resources for land acquisition and development of various park amenities.

2000 White House Millennium Council | Millennium Park was designated an official project of the White House Millennium Council by virtue of its ability to commemorate local history, reflect on current challenges, and prepare the community and its people for the 21st century.

HONOR THE PAST – IMAGINE THE FUTURE

2004 Millennium Park Dedication | The park was officially dedicated on July 2, 2004, at a festive event for the entire community. The Grand Opening Celebration was hosted by the Grand Rapids Jaycees and featured children's activities, speakers, and a Latin Jazz concert on the beach. The newly opened park offered visitors 1,100 feet of sandy beaches, a bathhouse, two playground areas, 20 grilling areas, and over 200 picnic tables.

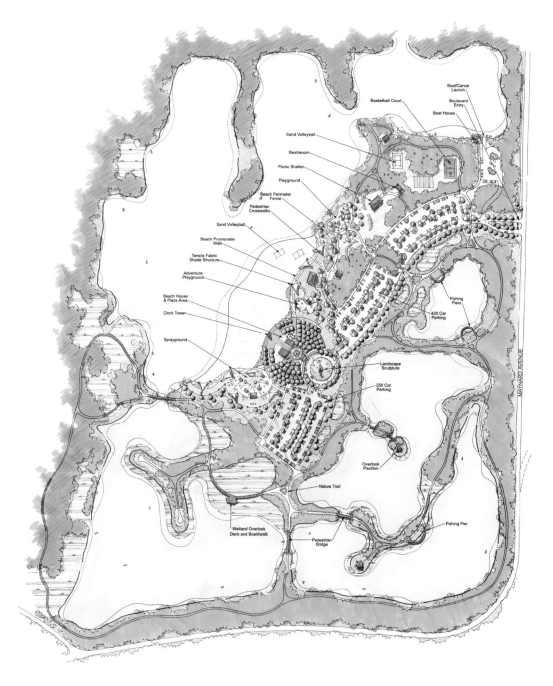

Boat/Canoe Launch
Basketball Court
Boulevard Entry
Boat House
Sand Volleyball
Restroom
Picnic Shelter
Playground
Beach Perimeter Fence
Pedestrian Crosswalks
Sand Volleyball
Fishing Piers
Beach Promenade Walk
420 Car Parking
Tensile Fabric Shade Structure
Adventure Playground
Beach House & Plaza Area
Clock Tower
Landscape Sculpture
Sprayground
250 Car Parking
Overlook Pavilion
Nature Trail
Wetland Overlook Deck and Boardwalk
Fishing Pier
Pedestrian Bridge

MAYNARD AVENUE

Recreation Core: 2003 Master Plan | The original 2003 Millennium Park Master Plan guided Phase I of the park's development. The plan described a Recreation Core that included a six-acre beach, splash pad, beach house, shelters, picnic areas, playgrounds, and fishing decks. Shown at right is the completed Recreation Core from above.

**Recreation Core: 2006
Splash Pad** | One of the park's most popular amenities, the splash pad is a magnet for families throughout the summer days. Designed for fun and safety, the area offers enough water activities to keep even the most active toddlers busy.

Recreation Core: 2006 Park Shelters

The four distinctive Millennium Park shelters are intentionally reminiscent of vintage Kent County park architecture. Incorporating wood, concrete, and limestone – indigenous materials – they provide a welcoming presence in the Recreation Core.

Two shelters are designed for large-size groups (125-person capacity); one is a medium-size group shelter (75-person capacity), which is located within the beach area, and another is a single-family shelter. Each shelter is equipped with picnic tables, charcoal grills, potable water, and electricity.

**Recreation Core: 2006
Public Beach and Lake**

| The Van Andel beach house features locker rooms, restrooms, and a busy concession stand. It overlooks a sprawling, man-made beach where crews trucked in enough beach-quality sand to cover six acres.

Recreation Core: 2006 Playground | The playground area offers swings, volleyball courts, and other play structures. It is a popular choice for children and teenagers.

Recreation Core: 2006 Fishing and Observation Decks

Prior to reclamation, the park quarries offered excellent fishing for a variety of panfish. In addition, the Parks Department "planted" over 1,200 large-mouth bass and hybrid bluegill in 2003, with another 10,000 bass, bluegill, and yellow perch in 2004. Yearly fish planting is planned. Two handicap-accessible decks provide easy access to the stocked ponds.

Recreation Core: 2006 Trails | Miles of paved, all-purpose trails and boardwalks wind through the park for cycling, walking, running, and in-line skating. The trail system makes its way through the emerging wetland environment that was created from the reclaimed land. The 15-mile Kent Trails system passes through Millennium Park on its route from John Ball Zoo to Byron Center.

Recreation Core: 2006 Gathering Place | Millennium Park has become one of Grand Rapids' premier locations for summertime reunions, picnics, and informal community meetings. No other local venue provides the range of recreational options offered within the park boundaries.

05

To Make a Circle | To make a circle,
You have to be willing
To walk backwards.

In a widening arc,
Through the unknown
To the familiar.

Finding your way,
You arrive at the truth
Having been there before.

Completing the Vision

Chapter 05 | In February 2005, the Millennium Park Architectural Advisory Board convened a Sustainable Design Committee to research and provide suggestions about how to restore the new park's ability to sustain plant, animal, and human life. The Sustainable Design Committee's efforts contributed to a comprehensive and visionary Millennium Park Master Plan Update, completed in November 2006. The new plan detailed how sustainable design concepts could be implemented at the park and incorporated them into a seven-point Millennium Standard, which will govern the ongoing management and long-term stewardship of the park.

The Millennium Standard | Millennium Park is being developed using two key sustainable design concepts: the ability of the park to be both financially self-sustaining and supportive of the long-term health of the land and its ecosystem, including people, plants, and animals. According to the updated Master Plan, "a secure, sustainable foundation will help Millennium Park endure as a place for respite, wonder, recreation, and renewal for the people of Kent County."

1. Recognize the interdependence of people and the environment.

Ecological Considerations
2. Restore ecological health and biodiversity.
3. Deploy integrated sustainable practices within and beyond Millennium Park.

Social Considerations
4. Offer a place for wholesome interaction accessible to all, especially our children.
5. Provide an inspirational setting for a range of recreational enjoyment.

Financial and Economic Considerations
6. Develop multi-benefit, multi-purpose Green Infrastructure elements.
7. Improve the local economy through sustainable practices.

All of the existing park features were re-evaluated within the renewed focus on sustainability. For instance, all new park construction will be governed by sustainable design and construction methods, including the US Green Building Council's LEED protocols. Landscapes throughout the park will be developed, restored, and stewarded as natural ecosystems. Wastewater on site will be treated and recycled; experiential learning opportunities will be created whenever possible; and the expansive regional trail system will be completed, with Millennium Park as a hub.

The Millennium Park Vision | The Millennium Park vision is to preserve, protect, and respect this gift of natural beauty and resources for the next generation. It will provide an exceptional recreational green space where people can connect with nature, and that is maintained in a spirit of stewardship and accessibility. Through a community-wide effort, Kent County will create a world-class, sustainable metropolitan park as a "gift to future generations" that provides green space that addresses recreational, environmental and social needs, and restores and preserves natural resources through collaborative public and private partnerships.

2008 Millennium Park Architectural Advisory Board members and staff, left to right: Robert Papp, Roger Sabine, Robert Mihos, board Chair Roger Morgan, Commissioner Richard VanderMolen, David Custer, Commissioner Arthur Tanis, Peter Secchia, Vern Ohlman, Francisco Vega, Mary Swanson, and Wesley Steer

Millennium Park Architectural Advisory Board | Originally started as an informal group to provide input on the design of amenities at Millennium Park, the Millennium Park Architectural Advisory Board was formally appointed in January 2004 to serve as a clearinghouse for ideas for park development and to ensure that future park projects were chosen and executed to be consistent with the Master Plan. The Board members represent cities within the boundaries of the park, the local design and business communities, and Kent County. Original members included Board Chair David Morren; Commissioner Roger Morgan as chair of the Finance and Physical Resources Committee; Commissioner Art Tanis, whose district encompasses a significant portion of the park; and Vern Ohlman, Francisco Vega, Peter Secchia and David Custer.

Left to right: Roger Sabine, Kent County Parks Director; Bill Stough, CEO Sustainable Research Group; Darwin Baas, Kent County Management Analyst; Vern Ohlman, Chairman of the Board, Senior Designer of Design Plus and Member of Millennium Park Architectural Advisory Board; Shirley Hubers, Hubers & Associates; Pat Hirdes, Manager of Central Services of Design One

Sustainable Design Committee | Led by Chair Vern Ohlman, the Sustainable Design Committee created a vision of Millennium Park as a model for future metropolitan parks around the world. According to Ohlman, "Millennium Park can help show the way to reversing eons of destructive abuse of our natural, life-sustaining environment."

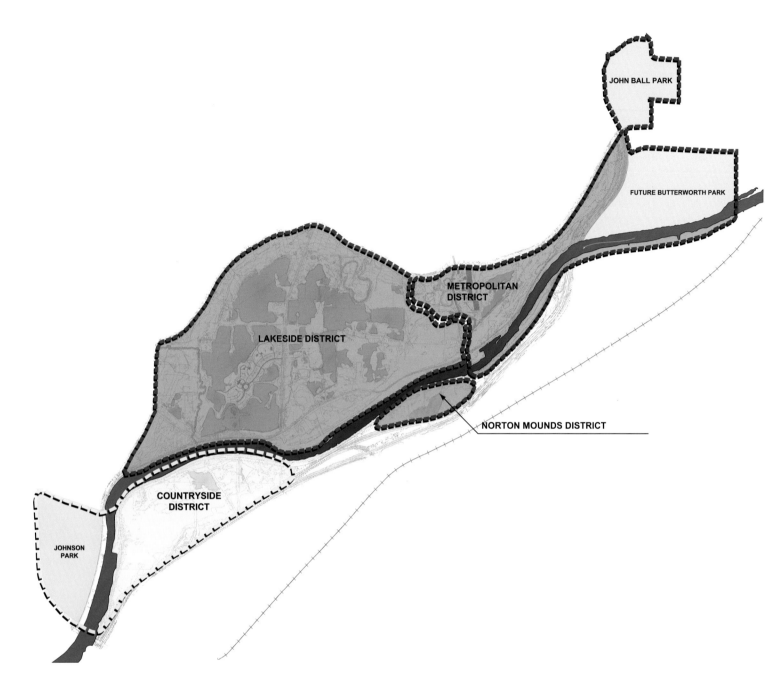

JOHN BALL PARK

FUTURE BUTTERWORTH PARK

METROPOLITAN DISTRICT

LAKESIDE DISTRICT

NORTON MOUNDS DISTRICT

COUNTRYSIDE DISTRICT

JOHNSON PARK

Four Distinct Park Districts | The updated Master Plan identifies four distinct districts, which are defined by their unique land features and man-made amenities.

- Metropolitan: urban community park
- Norton Mounds: sacred site
- Lakeside: series of lakes, ponds, and wetlands
- Countryside: rural, open landscape

Aerial view of Millennium Park in the spring of 2007

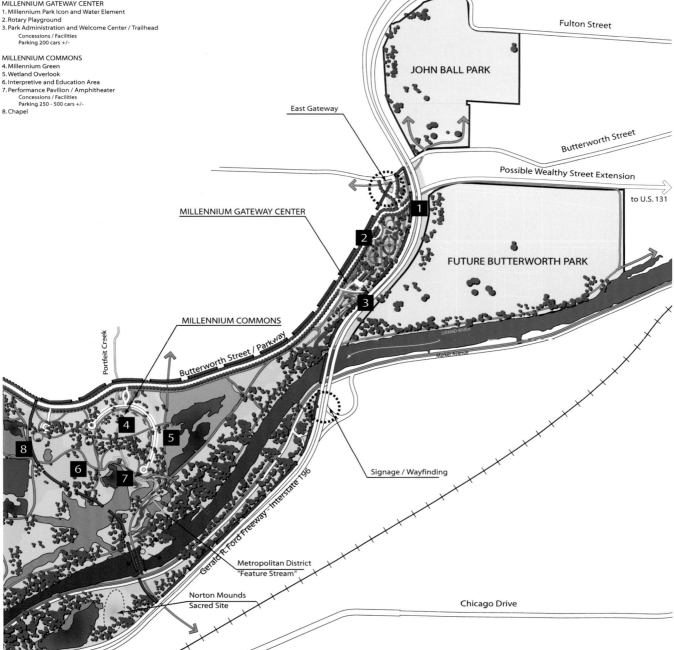

Legend

▬ ▬ ▬ District Boundary

MILLENNIUM GATEWAY CENTER
1. Millennium Park Icon and Water Element
2. Rotary Playground
3. Park Administration and Welcome Center / Trailhead
    Concessions / Facilities
    Parking 200 cars +/-

MILLENNIUM COMMONS
4. Millennium Green
5. Wetland Overlook
6. Interpretive and Education Area
7. Performance Pavilion / Amphitheater
    Concessions / Facilities
    Parking 250 - 500 cars +/-
8. Chapel

Fulton Street

JOHN BALL PARK

East Gateway

Butterworth Street

Possible Wealthy Street Extension

to U.S. 131

MILLENNIUM GATEWAY CENTER

1

2

FUTURE BUTTERWORTH PARK

3

MILLENNIUM COMMONS

Portfeit Creek

Butterworth Street / Parkway

GRAND RIVER

Market Avenue

4

5

8

6

7

Signage / Wayfinding

Gerald R. Ford Freeway - Interstate 196

Metropolitan District
"Feature Stream"

Norton Mounds
Sacred Site

Chicago Drive

Priority Park Features
Millennium
Gateway Center
(Metropolitan District)

The Gateway Center will be the most visible element of Millennium Park for generations to come. It provides a connection to the community and a link to other park facilities, such as John Ball Zoo and the future Butterworth Park. The proposed center would include these elements:

- Welcome Facility
- Trailhead
- Rotary International Playground
- Promenade
- Civic Plaza
- Administration Facility (green design)
- Water System (collect and re-use rainwater)
- East Gateway
- Parking

The Master Plan Update also recommends the creation of a unique, historically based "icon" at the center that will become a symbol for the entire park.

Legend

- District Boundary

RECREATION CORE (EXISTING)
9. Existing Beach House and Splash Pad
   Concessions / Facilities
   Parking 625 cars

THE MEADOW
10. Veteran's Grove
11. Large Group Picnic Area
    Concessions / Facilities
    Parking 300 cars +/-
12. River Access / Portage
13. Grand Overlook
14. Boating Center
    Kayak, Canoe Rentals
    Concessions / Facilities
    Parking 50 cars +/-

THE FEN
15. Interpretive Pavilion
    Trailhead
    Parking 50 cars +/-
    Facilities
16. Maintenance Building

Wooded Riparian Terrace	Open Water
Discharge Wetlands / Fen	Restored Prairie and Grassland
Wooded Seep	Restored Woodlands
Marsh	Restored Wetlands
Bluff Woodland	
Wooded Swamp	

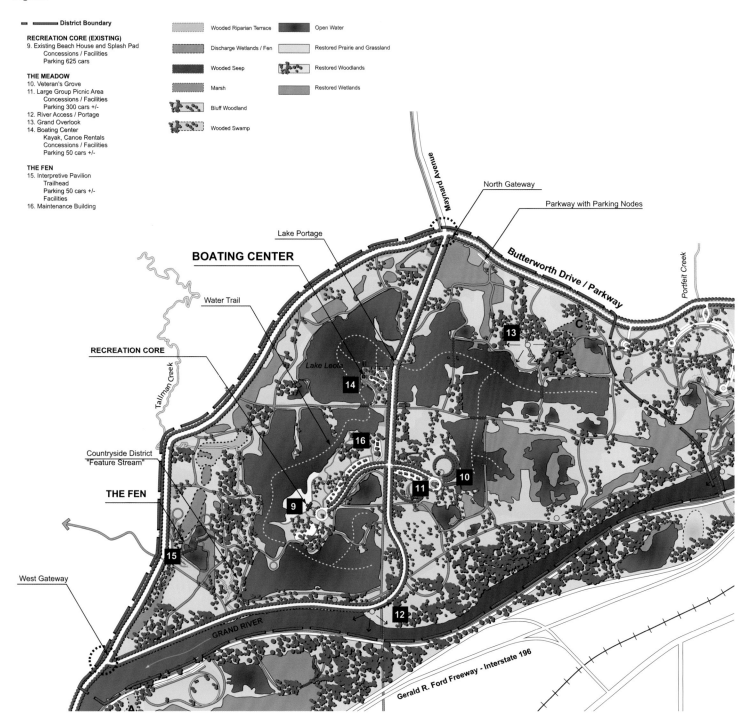

Priority Park Features
Boating Center
(Lakeside District)

Its various water features are the most distinctive elements of Millennium Park. The proposed Boating Center includes a building to house rental and lake-access facilities, concessions, parking, and a boat launch – along with shoreline rehabilitation and several bridge structures.

Legend

a. Trail connection to Recreation Core
b. Overlook
c. Naturalized shoreline and enhanced fish habitat
d. Rain gardens
e. Trail crossing - underpass
f. Sustainable paving demonstration
   Parking 50 cars +/-
g. Fen Pavilion
   Gathering space
   Restrooms
   Exhibits
h. Learn to fish areas
i. Interpretive trail
j. Prairie restoration and fen
k. Thin and restore woodland

Priority Park Features
The Fen
(Lakeside District)

The western edge of the Lakeside District includes a portion of the Fen, one of the park's richest remnant landscapes. Fens are wetlands fed by continuous groundwater that is rich in magnesium and calcium, making them home to several varieties of plants found in no other habitat. This area is going to be developed as a trailhead, with trails connecting to the beach and the regional trail system. It will also include several small, naturalized ponds for fishing.

Fred Meijer Millennium Trail Network | The Fred Meijer Millennium Trail Network was made possible through the generosity of Fred and Lena Meijer, whose significant lead gift kicked off the trail development project. Other major donations, as well as funding from Kent County, supported the acquisition of the final 114-acre parcel necessary to build the trail, and the development of significant features and areas throughout the trail network.

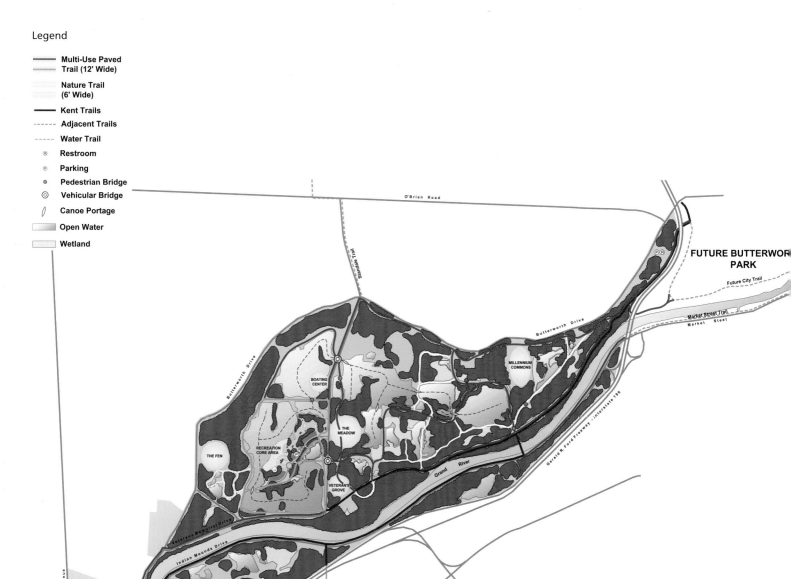

Legend

Multi-Use Paved
Trail (12' Wide)

Nature Trail
(6' Wide)

Kent Trails

Adjacent Trails

Water Trail

® Restroom

Ⓟ Parking

◉ Pedestrian Bridge

◎ Vehicular Bridge

∅ Canoe Portage

Open Water

Wetland

Priority Park Features | The planned Trail Network provides access to recreation
Fred Meijer Millennium areas as well as undeveloped natural areas. Walkers, cyclists
Trail Network and skaters also enjoy connections to community trail
systems, including Kent Trails.

A Circle | A circle gives everyone a place at the table.
A circle starts with tomorrow and ends up in yesterday.
A circle turns many voices into one.

A circle is a closed curve.
A circle never ends.

Author's Note | As soon as I started thinking deeply about the Millennium Park project, I began to see circles. The whole effort seemed to be about coming full circle, investing millions to return the land to its original state (or at least, a version of it). I'm not sure if the original peoples would recognize the area today, but I hope so. I tried to capture this sense of the lurking past in the poems. There are so many places in the park where it is possible to feel the presence of the people who came before us. There are actually scars left on the land from generations of use and abuse. I often imagined the first dwellers gathering thousands of years ago in this magnificent environment, enjoying the warm summer weather and each other's company. It's exactly what families are doing at the park today. That's the magic of this story.

Polly Hewitt

Very Special Thanks to:

Grand Rapids City Historian Emeritus, **Gordon Olson**, whose research, guidance, and passion for our community provided a solid foundation for this project.

The mother-son writing team of **Polly Hewitt** and **Harv Schaefer**, for their love of words and willingness to delve deeply into the Millennium Park vision.

ddm marketing & communications for their artistic vision, steady presence and dedication to making this book a reality.
www.teamddm.com

The extraordinarily talented team of photographers who captured the essence of Millennium Park:

Brian Kelly   Robert Neumann   Mary Taber-Lind
David Lubbers   Mitch Ranger   Andy Terzes

Unless otherwise noted, all the images and illustrations are from the collection and archives of the County of Kent, Michigan. Every effort has been made to contact photographers whose work can be identified, but many photographs in the archives of the County of Kent are unmarked. The page numbers on which a photographer's work can be found are noted below.

© **Brian Kelly**: Front cover and back cover, pages 1, 8, 38, 82 top left, 88 top left and middle right, 94 middle right, 95 bottom left, 96 bottom right, 97 top row, center left and bottom, 98 middle right, 100-101, 120, 124-125
www.briankellyphoto.net

© **David Lubbers:** pages 16-17, 34-35, 58-59, 80-81, 106-107
www.davidlubbers.com

© **Robert Neumann**: pages 2-7, 20, 29 bottom right, 41, 53, 78-79, 82 top and bottom right, 84, 86, 92-93, 94 top right, 96 top right, 99, 109, 111, 112, 117
www.bigeventstudios.com

© **Mitch Ranger**: pages 10, 32-33, 82 middle right, 87, 99 middle right, 102-103, 113, 123, 126-127
www.bigeventstudios.com

© **Mary Taber-Lind**: pages 62, 83, 88, 89, 94 bottom left and right, top right, 95, 96 top, middle and bottom left, 97 center and bottom right, 98, 104-105, 110

© **Andy Terzes**: pages 11 four, seven, nine and eleven o'clock, 36-37, 39, 44-45, 52, 56-57, 60
www.terzesphoto.com

© **Grand Rapids Public Library, Reyerson Library**: pages 42-43, 46-51

© **Public Museum of Grand Rapids**, Michigan. Photographer, Thomas Kachadurian: page 28

© **Public Museum of Grand Rapids**, Michigan: pages 18, 29, 54-55

© **TJ Hamilton,** Fifth Third River Bank Run: page 99 bottom right